FY 2015 Police and Youth Engagement: Supporting the Role of Law Enforcement in Juvenile Justice Reform

OJJDP-2015-4217

Contents

FY 2015 Police and Youth Engagement: Supporting the Role of Law Enforcement in Juvenile Justice Reform

A. Program Description

Overview

The Office of Juvenile Justice and Delinquency Prevention (OJJDP) provides national leadership, coordination, and resources to prevent and respond to juvenile delinquency and victimization. To fulfill this mission, OJJDP collaborates with professionals from diverse disciplines to improve juvenile justice practices and policies.

Recent events have focused national attention on the need for enhanced trust between local law enforcement and the communities that they serve. OJJDP seeks to help inform law enforcement executives of key juvenile justice issues that jurisdictions face in improving relations between youth and law enforcement. Specifically, OJJDP will examine how to foster strong, collaborative relationships between local law enforcement, youth, families, and communities. OJJDP will emphasize evidence-based practices specific to youth engagement and will identify areas within police operations where additional training and technical assistance are needed, including training and protocols to enable law enforcement to better identify and respond to children who have been direct victims of or witnesses to violence in their homes, schools, and/or communities.

This program is authorized pursuant to Section 221 of the Juvenile Justice and Delinquency Prevention Act, 42 U.S.C. § 5631.

Program-Specific Information

Trust between law enforcement agencies and the people they protect and serve is essential in a democracy. It is key to the stability of communities, the integrity of the criminal and juvenile justice systems, and the safe and effective delivery of policing services. Law enforcement has a critical role to play in juvenile justice reform. For many youth in need of services, law enforcement is the initial point of contact. For this reason, it is important that law enforcement develops tools to address juvenile crime that are effective and developmentally appropriate. Additionally, law enforcement is uniquely positioned to play an active role in changing community norms and establishing policies that better support youth and families.

This solicitation will provide funding to an eligible applicant to support the convening of a youth and law enforcement roundtable and development of an institute on best practices and innovative approaches relating to law enforcement, youth, and juvenile justice. The successful applicant will support an initial roundtable and one institute during the initial 12-month award period to include planning and implementation.

OJJDP is seeking programs that address youth and law enforcement partnerships in these categories:

- youth who are at risk of or involved in gang activity (to include youth who are siblings of gang-involved youth and youth living in communities with high levels of gang activity).

- youth living in communities with high levels of handgun violence.

- youth who are exposed to or witnesses of family, school, and/or community violence.

- girls who are at risk of involvement or involved in the juvenile justice system.

Goals, Objectives, and Deliverables

This project will fund the successful applicant to provide training and technical assistance in support of a youth and law enforcement roundtable and a Law Enforcement Leadership Institute on Juvenile Justice. These components are described below:

- **Youth and law enforcement roundtable.** OJJDP, with support from the training and technical assistance provider, will convene a roundtable discussion on enhancing the infrastructure to support, sustain, and expand youth and law enforcement engagement. Invitees will include a cross section of national law enforcement organizations and federal partners. Specifically, the roundtable will inform OJJDP of specific components to consider, including recommendations on how to structure the Law Enforcement Leadership Institute on Juvenile Justice. Virtual meetings will occur post-roundtable, and a report will be developed.

- **Law Enforcement Leadership Institute on Juvenile Justice.** Based on the youth and law enforcement roundtable, this leadership institute will immerse law enforcement executives in best practices and innovative approaches on how to improve interactions between youth and law enforcement and effectively contribute to juvenile justice reform. Participants will learn how to change the culture within their agencies and support collaboration with other public and private organizations. State and local law enforcement executives will explore their role as change agents and determine how they can more effectively address systemic juvenile justice issues, improve local responses to justice-involved youth, and accelerate progress toward more successful outcomes for youth, families, and communities. Topics may include, but are not limited to, the following:

  o cultural transformation in law enforcement agencies—policies, practices, and protocols that support juvenile justice reform.

  o adolescent development and implications for law enforcement.

  o children's exposure to violence in their homes, schools, and communities.

  o complying with the core protections of the Juvenile Justice and Delinquency Prevention Act.

  o eliminating racial and ethnic disparities.

- partnerships to address adolescents' mental health, substance abuse, and trauma needs.

- diversion and risk assessment.

- law enforcement and school collaborations.

- data collection and information sharing.

- advocating for community reforms.

The goals of this program are to:

- improve law enforcement's ability to identify and respond to children who have been exposed to violence in their homes, schools, and/or communities.

- improve law enforcement agencies' response to justice-involved youth and at-risk youth.

- promote enhanced law enforcement collaboration on juvenile justice reform in communities.

- demonstrate the efficacy of evidence-based practices and principles to improve the delivery of services (e.g. alternatives to detention, diversion for status offenders, adoption of policies or standard operating procedures that support juvenile justice reform).

The objectives of this program are as follows:

- introduce law enforcement agencies to best practices and innovative approaches related to juvenile justice reform and work closely with those agencies to assess their current response to youth.

- develop agency-specific action plans subsequent to their participation in the institute.

- develop, implement, and enhance training and technical assistance materials and activities relevant to police and youth engagement.

- provide training and technical assistance to grantees that will build capacity, assess needs, initiate strategic planning, implement appropriate program improvements, evaluate program performance, and help sustain their programs.

The program narrative should reflect how the applicant will accomplish the program objectives through the proposed deliverables. Applicants should be realistic in estimating the cost of deliverables and in detailing the implementation schedule. OJJDP also encourages applicants to be innovative and to propose alternative approaches to the delivery of training and technical assistance to maximize resources.

Youth engagement. Youth engagement can be achieved by (1) actively engaging justice-involved youth and individuals formerly incarcerated as youth in planning and decision-making that affects their individual outcomes and (2) giving them a voice in the development of policies, practices, and governance of the agency or systems in which they are involved. OJJDP seeks to actively engage and partner with justice-involved youth and their families to inform programs and policies.

Family engagement. OJJDP envisions a transformed juvenile justice system that recognizes and builds upon the strengths, values, and diversity of families and communities to best serve the children and youth who come into contact with the system and to improve both safety and quality of life for all. This system will honor and support families before, during, and after their children have contact with the system.

Applicants should describe how the proposed program will include both a youth engagement and a family engagement component.

OJJDP training and technical assistance awardee standards. OJJDP has developed the *Core Performance Standards for Training, Technical Assistance, and Evaluation* to promote among providers the consistency and quality of OJJDP-sponsored training and technical assistance and to advance common expectations of performance excellence. The standards present minimum expectations that providers must meet for effective practice in the planning, coordination, delivery, and evaluation of training. Award recipients must coordinate with OJJDP's National Training and Technical Assistance Center (NTTAC) in the assessment and delivery of services to ensure the effective use of OJJDP grant funding. For additional information, go to OJJDP's NTTAC website.

Requirements related to coordination of activities will include, but are not limited to:

- **Coordination with OJJDP NTTAC.** OJJDP requires all training and technical assistance projects to coordinate their activities with OJJDP NTTAC by complying with all OJJDP NTTAC protocols to ensure coordinated delivery of services among providers and effective use of OJJDP grant funding. OJJDP reserves the right to modify these protocols at any time with reasonable notice to the grantee prior to project completion.

- **OJJDP-funded webinars.** The award recipient must comply with OJJDP's Webinar Guidelines, as described in the core performance standards. Minimally, OJJDP training and technical assistance providers will submit to OJJDP NTTAC information in advance of all events for the online calendar, use the approved OJJDP presentation template, and record events and upload the files onto NTTAC's Online University.

- **Training information sharing.** The Office of Justice Programs (OJP) will be collecting information from its program offices on OJP-funded training and technical assistance events. Award recipients must use OJJDP's standard electronic training request form and submit information to NTTAC on all training events (i.e. name of requestor, description of request, dates of event etc.) 30 days in advance of the event date and report additional data as OJJDP requires.

Evidence-based programs or practices. OJJDP encourages applicants to become familiar with the resources found on the OJP CrimeSolutions.gov and OJJDP Model Programs Guide websites to find information about evidence-based programs in criminal justice, juvenile justice, and crime victim services.

OJP strongly emphasizes the use of data and evidence in policy making and program development in criminal justice, juvenile justice, and crime victim services. OJP is committed to:

- improving the quantity and quality of evidence OJP generates;
- integrating evidence into program, practice, and policy decisions within OJP and the field; and
- improving the translation of evidence into practice.

OJP considers programs and practices to be evidence-based when their effectiveness has been demonstrated by causal evidence, generally obtained through one or more outcome evaluations. Causal evidence documents a relationship between an activity or intervention (including technology) and its intended outcome, including measuring the direction and size of a change, and the extent to which a change may be attributed to the activity or intervention. Causal evidence depends on the use of scientific methods to rule out, to the extent possible, alternative explanations for the documented change. The strength of causal evidence, based on the factors described above, will influence the degree to which OJP considers a program or practice to be evidence-based.

Additional resources. OJJDP encourages applicants to review the recommendations from the Attorney General's National Task Force on Children Exposed to Violence and the Attorney General's Advisory Committee on American Indian/Alaska Native Children Exposed to Violence and the National Research Council's *Reforming Juvenile Justice: A Developmental Approach* and *Implementing Juvenile Justice Reform* and consider incorporating the recommendations into their applications, where applicable.

B. Federal Award Information

OJJDP expects to make one cooperative agreement for as much as $400,000 for a 12-month project period, beginning on October 1, 2015.

Based on the availability of funds and determination of successful performance, OJJDP may provide annual continuation funding for as many as 2 additional years under this solicitation. Important considerations in decisions regarding supplemental funding include, among other factors, the availability of funding, strategic priorities, assessment of the quality of the management of the award (for example, timeliness and quality of progress reports), and assessment of the progress of the work funded under the award.

All awards are subject to the availability of appropriated funds and to any modifications or additional requirements that may be imposed by law.

Type of award[1]. OJJDP expects to make any award from this solicitation in the form of a cooperative agreement, which is a particular type of grant used if OJJDP expects to have ongoing substantial involvement in award activities. Substantial involvement includes direct oversight and involvement with the grantee organization in implementation of the grant but does not involve day-to-day project management. See Administrative, National Policy, and

---

[1] See generally 31 U.S.C. §§ 6301-6305 (defines and describes various forms of federal assistance relationships, including grants and cooperative agreements (a type of grant)).

other Legal Requirements, under Section F. Federal Award Administration, for details regarding the federal involvement anticipated under an award from this solicitation.

Financial management and system of internal controls. If selected for funding, the award recipient must:

(a) Establish and maintain effective internal control over the federal award that provides reasonable assurance that the nonfederal entity is managing the federal award in compliance with federal statutes, regulations, and the terms and conditions of the federal award. These internal controls should be in compliance with guidance in "Standards for Internal Control in the Federal Government" issued by the Comptroller General of the United States and the "Internal Control Integrated Framework", issued by the Committee of Sponsoring Organizations of the Treadway Commission (COSO).

(b) Comply with federal statutes, regulations, and the terms and conditions of the federal awards.

(c) Evaluate and monitor the nonfederal entity's compliance with statute, regulations, and the terms and conditions of federal awards.

(d) Take prompt action when instances of noncompliance are identified, including noncompliance identified in audit findings.

(e) Take reasonable measures to safeguard protected personally identifiable information and other information the federal awarding agency or pass-through entity designates as sensitive or the nonfederal entity considers sensitive consistent with applicable federal, state, and local laws regarding privacy and obligations of confidentiality.

In order to better understand administrative requirements and cost principles, award applicants are encouraged to enroll, at no charge, in the Department of Justice Grants Financial Management Online Training available here.

Budget Information

Cost sharing or match requirement. This solicitation does not require a match. However, if a successful application proposes a voluntary match amount, and OJP approves the budget, the total match amount incorporated into the approved budget becomes mandatory and subject to audit.

Preagreement cost approvals. OJP does not typically approve preagreement costs; an applicant must request and obtain the prior written approval of OJP for all such costs. If approved, preagreement costs could be paid from grant funds consistent with a grantee's approved budget, and under applicable cost standards. However, all such costs prior to award and prior to approval of the costs are incurred at the sole risk of an applicant. Generally, no applicant should incur project costs *before* submitting an application requesting federal funding for those costs. Should there be extenuating circumstances that appear to be appropriate for OJP's consideration as preagreement costs, the applicant should contact the point of contact listed on the title page of this announcement for details on the requirements for submitting a written request for approval. See the section on Costs Requiring Prior Approval in the Financial Guide, for more information.

Limitation on use of award funds for employee compensation; waiver. With respect to any award of more than $250,000 made under this solicitation, recipients may not use federal funds to pay total cash compensation (salary plus cash bonuses) to any employee of the award recipient at a rate that exceeds 110 percent of the maximum annual salary payable to a member of the Federal Government's Senior Executive Service (SES) at an agency with a Certified SES Performance Appraisal System for that year.[2] The 2015 salary table for SES employees is available at the Office of Personnel Management website. Note: A recipient may compensate an employee at a greater rate, provided the amount in excess of this compensation limitation is paid with non-federal funds. (Any such additional compensation will not be considered matching funds where match requirements apply.)

The Assistant Attorney General for OJP may exercise discretion to waive, on an individual basis, the limitation on compensation rates allowable under an award. An applicant requesting a waiver should include a detailed justification in the budget narrative of the application. Unless the applicant submits a waiver request and justification with the application, the applicant should anticipate that OJP will request the applicant to adjust and resubmit the budget.

The justification should include the particular qualifications and expertise of the individual, the uniqueness of the service the individual will provide, the individual's specific knowledge of the program or project being undertaken with award funds, and a statement explaining that the individual's salary is commensurate with the regular and customary rate for an individual with his/her qualifications and expertise, and for the work to be done.

Prior approval, planning, and reporting of conference/meeting/training costs. OJP strongly encourages applicants that propose to use award funds for any conference-, meeting-, or training-related activity to review carefully – before submitting an application – the OJP policy and guidance on conference approval, planning, and reporting. OJP policy and guidance (1) encourage minimization of conference, meeting, and training costs; (2) require prior written approval (which may affect project timelines) of most such costs for cooperative agreement recipients and of some such costs for grant recipients; and (3) set cost limits, including a general prohibition of all food and beverage costs.

Costs associated with language assistance (if applicable). If an applicant proposes a program or activity that would deliver services or benefits to individuals, the costs of taking reasonable steps to provide meaningful access to those services or benefits for individuals with limited English proficiency may be allowable. Reasonable steps to provide meaningful access to services or benefits may include interpretation or translation services where appropriate.

For additional information, see the "Civil Rights Compliance" section under "Solicitation Requirements" in the OJP Funding Resource Center.

C. Eligibility Information

For additional eligibility information, see the title page.

---

[2] This limitation on use of award funds does not apply to the non-profit organizations specifically named at Appendix VIII to 2 C.F.R. part 200.

Cost sharing or match requirement. For additional information on cost sharing and match requirement, see Section B. Federal Award Information.

Limit on number of application submissions. If an applicant submits multiple versions of the same application, OJJDP will review only the most recent system-validated version submitted. For more information on system-validated versions, see How To Apply.

D. Application and Submission Information

What an Application Should Include

Applicants should anticipate that if they fail to submit an application that contains all of the specified elements, it may negatively affect the review of their application; and, should a decision be made to make an award, it may result in the inclusion of special conditions that preclude the recipient from accessing or using award funds pending satisfaction of the conditions.

Moreover, applicants should anticipate that applications that are determined to be nonresponsive to the scope of the solicitation, do not request funding within the funding limit, or that do not include the application elements that OJJDP has designated to be critical, will neither proceed to peer review nor receive further consideration. Under this solicitation, OJJDP has designated the following application elements as critical: Program Narrative, Budget Detail Worksheet or Budget Narrative.

Applicants should review the "Note on File Names and File Types" under How To Apply to be sure that they submit their applications in the permitted formats.

OJP strongly recommends that applicants use appropriately descriptive file names (e.g., "Program Narrative," "Budget Detail Worksheet and Budget Narrative," "Timelines," "Memoranda of Understanding," "Resumes") for all attachments. Also, OJP recommends that applicants include resumes in a single file.

1. Information to Complete the Application for Federal Assistance (SF-424)

The SF-424 is a required standard form used as a cover sheet for submission of pre-applications, applications, and related information. Grants.gov and OJP's Grants Management System (GMS) take information from the applicant's profile to populate the fields on this form. When selecting "type of applicant," if the applicant is a for-profit entity, select "For-Profit Organization" or "Small Business" (as applicable).

Intergovernmental review. This funding opportunity is subject to Executive Order 12372. Applicants may find the names and addresses of their state's Single Point of Contact (SPOC) at the following website: www.whitehouse.gov/omb/grants_spoc/. Applicants whose state appears on the SPOC list must contact their state's SPOC to find out about, and comply with, the state's process under Executive Order 12372. In completing the SF-424, applicants whose state appears on the SPOC list are to make the appropriate selection in response to question 19 once the applicant has complied with their state's E.O. 12372 process. (Applicants whose state does not appear on the SPOC list are to make the appropriate selection in response to question 19 to indicate that the "Program is subject to E.O. 12372 but has not been selected by the State for review.")

2. Project Abstract

Applications should include a high-quality project abstract that summarizes the proposed project in 400 words or less. Project abstracts should be—

- written for a general public audience.
- submitted as a separate attachment with "Project Abstract" as part of its file name.
- single-spaced, using a standard 12-point font (Times New Roman) with 1-inch margins.

As a separate attachment, the project abstract will **not** count against the page limit for the program narrative.

The abstract should briefly describe the project's purpose, the population to be served, and the activities that the applicant will implement to achieve the project's goals and objectives. The abstract should describe how the applicant will measure progress toward these goals. The abstract should indicate whether the applicant will use any portion of the project budget to conduct research as described in Note on Project Evaluations on page 15.

3. Program Narrative

Applicants must submit a program narrative that presents a detailed description of the purpose, goals, objectives, strategies, design, and management of the proposed program. The program narrative should be double-spaced with 1-inch margins, not exceeding 30 pages of 8½ by 11 inches, and use a standard 12-point font, preferably Times New Roman. Pages should be numbered "1 of 30," etc. The tables, charts, pictures, etc., including all captions, legends, keys, subtext, etc., may be single-spaced and will count in the 30-page limit. Material required under the Budget and Budget Narrative and Additional Attachments sections will not count toward the program narrative page count. Applicants may provide bibliographical references as a separate attachment that will not count toward the 30-page program narrative limit. If the program narrative fails to comply with these length-related restrictions, OJJDP may consider such noncompliance in peer review and in final award decisions.

The program narrative should address the following selection criteria: (1) statement of the problem; (2) goals, objectives, and performance measures; (3) program design and implementation; and (4) capabilities/competencies. The applicant should clearly delineate the connections between and among each of these sections. For example, the applicant should derive the goals and objectives directly from the problems to be addressed. Similarly, the project design section should clearly explain how the program's structure and activities will accomplish the goals and objectives identified in the previous section.

The following sections should be included as part of the program narrative:

a. **Statement of the problem.** Applicants should briefly describe the nature and scope of the problem that the program will address (e.g., need for improved public trust in law enforcement, children exposed to violence, gang activity, need for alternative programs in schools, lack of family and youth engagement, etc.). The applicant should use data to provide evidence that the problem exists, demonstrate the size and scope of the problem, and document the effects of the problem on the target population and the larger community. Applicants should describe the target population and any previous or current attempts to address the problem.

Applicants should describe any research or evaluation studies that relate to the problem and contribute to the applicant's understanding of its causes and potential solutions. While OJJDP expects applicants to review the research literature for relevant studies, they should also explore whether unpublished local sources of research or evaluation data are available.

b. **Goals, objectives, and performance measures.** Applicants should describe the goals of the proposed program and identify its objectives. When formulating the program's goals and objectives, applicants should be cognizant of the performance measures that OJJDP will require successful applicants to provide.

Goals. Applicants should describe the program's intent to change, reduce, or eliminate the problem noted in the previous section and outline the project's goals.

Program objectives. Applicants should explain how the program will accomplish its goals. Objectives are specific, quantifiable statements of the project's desired results. They should be clearly linked to the problem identified in the preceding section and measurable.

Performance measures. To assist the Department with fulfilling its responsibilities under the Government Performance and Results Act of 1993 (GPRA), Public Law 103-62, and the GPRA Modernization Act of 2010, Public Law 111–352, applicants that receive funding under this solicitation must provide data that measure the results of their work done under this solicitation. OJP will require any award recipient, post award, to provide the data requested in the "Data Grantee Provides" column so that OJP can calculate values for the "Performance Measures" column. OJJDP will require award recipients to submit semiannual performance metrics of relevant data through the Data Reporting Tool (DCTAT) located at www.ojjdp-dctat.org/. Performance measures for this solicitation are as follows:

Objective	Performance Measure(s)	Description	Data Grantee Provides
To develop, implement, and enhance training and technical materials and activities that support enhanced collaboration relevant to police and youth engagement.	Number of training requests received.	This measure represents the number of training requests received during the reporting period. Requests can come from individuals or organizations served.	Number of training requests received during the reporting period.
	Number of technical assistance requests received.	This measure represents the number of technical assistance requests received during the reporting period. Requests can come from individuals or organizations served.	Number of technical assistance requests received during the reporting period.

	Number of program materials developed during the reporting period.	This measure represents the number of program materials that were developed during the reporting period. Include only substantive materials such as program overviews, client workbooks, lists of local service providers. Do not include program advertisements or administrative forms such as sign-in sheets or client tracking forms. Count the number of pieces developed. Program records are the preferred data source.	Number of program materials developed.
	Number of planning or training events held during the reporting period.	This measure represents the number of planning or training activities held during the reporting period. Planning and training activities include creation of task forces or interagency committees, meetings held, needs assessments undertaken, etc. Preferred data source is program records.	Number of planning or training activities held during the reporting period.
	Number of people trained during the reporting period.	This measure represents the number of people trained during the reporting period. The number is the raw number of people receiving any formal training relevant to the program or their position as program staff. Include any training from any source or medium received during the reporting period as long as receipt of training can be verified. Training does not have to have been completed during the reporting period. Preferred data source is program records.	Number of people trained.
	Number of program policies changed, improved, or rescinded during the reporting period.	This measure represents the number of cross-program or agency policies or procedures changed, improved, or rescinded during the reporting period. A policy is a plan or specific course of action that guides the general goals and directives of programs and/or agencies. Include polices that are relevant to the topic area of the program or that affect program operations. Preferred data source is program records.	Number of program policies changed during the reporting period. Number of program policies rescinded during the reporting period.
	Percentage of people exhibiting an increased knowledge of the program area during the reporting period.	This measure represents the number of people who exhibit an increased knowledge of the program area after participating in training. Use of pre- and post-tests is preferred.	Number of people exhibiting an increase in knowledge post-training.

			Number of people trained during the reporting period.
	Percentage of organizations reporting improvements in operations based on training and technical assistance.	The number and percentage of organizations reporting improvements in operations as a result of training and technical assistance 1 to 6 months post-service. For example, enhanced collaborative efforts sustained should be included (e.g. alternatives to detention, diversion for status offenders, adoption of policies or standard operating procedures in support of juvenile justice reform).	The number of organizations reporting improvements in operations based on training and technical assistance during the reporting period.

Number of organizations served by training and technical assistance during the reporting period. |
| | Percentage of those served by training and technical assistance who reported implementing an evidence-based program and/or practice during or after the training and technical assistance. | Number and percentage of programs served by training and technical assistance that reported implementing an evidence-based program and/or practice during or after the training and technical assistance. Evidence-based programs and practices include program models that have been shown, through rigorous evaluation and replication, to be effective at preventing or reducing juvenile delinquency or related risk factors, such as substance use. | Number of programs served by training and technical assistance that reported using an evidence-based program and / or practice.

Number of programs served by training and technical assistance. |
| | Number of program materials disseminated during the reporting period. | This measure represents the number of program materials disseminated during the reporting period. | Enter the number of program materials disseminated during the reporting period |

OJJDP does not require applicants to submit performance measures data with their application. Performance measures are included as an alert that OJJDP will require successful applicants to submit specific data as part of their reporting requirements. For the application, applicants should indicate an understanding of these requirements and discuss how they will gather the required data, should they receive funding.

OJJDP encourages award recipients to use information from existing program records to fulfill performance measures reporting requirements rather than initiating new data collection activities for this purpose.

Note on project evaluations. Applicants that propose to use funds awarded through this solicitation to conduct project evaluations should be aware that certain project evaluations (such as systematic investigations designed to develop or contribute to generalizable knowledge) may constitute "research" for purposes of applicable DOJ human subjects protection regulations. However, project evaluations that are intended only to generate internal improvements to a program or service, or are conducted only to meet OJP's performance measure data reporting requirements likely do not constitute "research." Applicants should provide sufficient information for OJP to determine whether the particular project they propose would either intentionally or unintentionally collect and/or use information in such a way that it meets the DOJ regulatory definition of research.

Research, for the purposes of human subjects protections for OJP-funded programs, is defined as, "a systematic investigation, including research development, testing, and evaluation, designed to develop or contribute to generalizable knowledge" 28 C.F.R. § 46.102(d). For additional information on determining whether a proposed activity would constitute research, see the decision tree to assist applicants on the "Research and the Protection of Human Subjects" section of the OJP Funding Resource Center webpage. Applicants whose proposals may involve a research or statistical component also should review the "Data Privacy and Confidentiality Requirements" section on that webpage.

c. **Project design and implementation.** Applicants should detail how the project will operate throughout the funding period and describe the strategies that they will use to achieve the goals and objectives identified in the previous section. Applicants should describe how they will complete the deliverables stated in the Goals, Objectives, and Deliverables section on page 5. OJJDP encourages applicants to select evidence-based practices for their programs.

This section should also include details regarding any leveraged resources (cash or in-kind) from local sources to support the project and discuss plans for sustainability beyond the grant period.

Logic model. Applicants should include a logic model that graphically illustrates how the performance measures are related to the project's problems, goals, objectives, and design. See sample logic models here. Applicants should submit the logic model as a separate attachment, as stipulated in Additional Attachments, page 19.

Timeline. Applicants should submit a realistic timeline or milestone chart that indicates major tasks associated with the goals and objectives of the project, assigns responsibility for each, and plots completion of each task by month or quarter for the duration of the award, using "Year 1," "Month 1," "Quarter 1," etc., not calendar dates (see "Sample Project Timelines" here.).

Applicants should submit the timeline as a separate attachment, as stipulated in Additional Attachments, page 19. On receipt of an award, the recipient may revise the timeline, based on training and technical assistance that OJJDP will provide.

d. **Capabilities and competencies.** This section should describe the experience and capability of the applicant organization and any contractors or subgrantees that the applicant will use to implement and manage this effort and its associated federal funding, highlighting any previous experience implementing projects of similar design or magnitude. Applicants should highlight their experience/capability/capacity to manage subawards, including details on their system for fiscal accountability.

Management and staffing patterns should be clearly connected to the project design described in the previous section. Applicants should describe the roles and responsibilities of project staff and explain the program's organizational structure and operations. Applicants should include a copy of an organizational chart showing how the organization operates, including who manages the finances; how the organization manages subawards, if there are any; and the management of the project proposed for funding.

Letters of support/memoranda of understanding. If submitting a joint application, as described under Eligibility, page 1, applicants should provide signed and dated letters of support or memoranda of understanding for all key partners that include the following:

* expression of support for the program and a statement of willingness to participate and collaborate with it.

* description of the partner's current role and responsibilities in the planning process and expected responsibilities when the program is operational.

* estimate of the percentage of time that the partner will devote to the planning and operation of the project.

4. **Budget Detail Worksheet and Budget Narrative**

Applicants should provide a budget that (1) is complete, allowable, and cost-effective in relation to the proposed activities; (2) shows the cost calculations demonstrating how they arrived at the total amount requested; and (3) provides a brief supporting narrative to link costs with project activities. The budget should cover the entire award period.

For questions pertaining to budget and examples of allowable and unallowable costs, see the Financial Guide.

a. **Budget Detail Worksheet.** Find a sample Budget Detail Worksheet here. Applicants that submit their budget in a different format should include the budget categories listed in the sample budget worksheet.

b. **Budget Narrative.** The budget narrative should thoroughly and clearly describe every category of expense listed in the Budget Detail Worksheet. OJP expects proposed budgets to be complete, cost effective, and allowable (e.g., reasonable, allocable, and necessary for project activities).

Applicants should demonstrate in their budget narratives how they will maximize cost effectiveness of grant expenditures. Budget narratives should generally describe cost effectiveness in relation to potential alternatives and the goals of the project. For example, a budget narrative should detail why planned in-person meetings are necessary, or how technology and collaboration with outside organizations could be used to reduce costs, without compromising quality.

The narrative should be mathematically sound and correspond with the information and figures provided in the Budget Detail Worksheet. The narrative should explain how the applicant estimated and calculated all costs, and how they are relevant to the completion of the proposed project. The narrative may include tables for clarification purposes but need not be in a spreadsheet format. As with the Budget Detail Worksheet, the Budget Narrative should be broken down by year.

c. **Noncompetitive procurement contracts in excess of simplified acquisition threshold.** If an applicant proposes to make one or more noncompetitive procurements of products or services, where the noncompetitive procurement will exceed the simplified acquisition threshold (also known as the small purchase threshold), which is currently set at $150,000, the application should address the considerations outlined in the Financial Guide.

d. **Preagreement cost approvals.** For information on preagreement costs, see Section B. Federal Award Information.

5. **Indirect Cost Rate Agreement (if applicable)**

Indirect costs are allowed only if the applicant has a current federally approved indirect cost rate. (This requirement does not apply to units of local government.) Attach a copy of the federally approved indirect cost rate agreement to the application. Applicants that do not have an approved rate may request one through their cognizant federal agency, which will review all documentation and approve a rate for the applicant organization, or, if the applicant's accounting system permits, costs may be allocated in the direct cost categories. For the definition of Cognizant Federal Agency, see the "Glossary of Terms" in the Financial Guide. For assistance with identifying your cognizant agency, contact the Customer Service Center at 1-800-458-0786 or at ask.ocfo@usdoj.gov. If DOJ is the cognizant federal agency, applicants may obtain information needed to submit an indirect cost rate proposal here.

6. **Applicant Disclosure of High Risk Status**

Applicants are to disclose whether they are currently designated high risk by another federal grant making agency. This includes any status requiring additional oversight by the federal agency due to past programmatic or financial concerns. If an applicant is designated high risk by another federal grant making agency, you must email the following information to OJPComplianceReporting@usdoj.gov at the time of application submission:

- The federal agency that currently designated the applicant as high risk;
- Date the applicant was designated high risk;
- The high risk point of contact name, phone number, and email address, from that federal agency; and
- Reasons for the high risk status.

OJP seeks this information to ensure appropriate federal oversight of any grant award. Unlike the Excluded Parties List, this high risk information does not disqualify any organization from receiving an OJP award. However, additional grant oversight may be included, if necessary, in award documentation.

7. Additional Attachments

Applicants should submit the following information, as stipulated in the cited pages, as attachments to their applications. While the materials listed below are not assigned specific point values, peer reviewers will, as appropriate, consider these items when rating applications. For example, reviewers will consider résumés and/or letters of support/ memoranda of understanding when assessing "capabilities/competencies." Peer reviewers will not consider any additional information that the applicant submits other than that specified below.

a. **Applicant disclosure of pending applications.** Applicants are to disclose whether they have pending applications for federally funded grants or subgrants (including cooperative agreements) that include requests for funding to support the same project being proposed under this solicitation and will cover the identical cost items outlined in the budget narrative and worksheet in the application under this solicitation. The disclosure should include both direct applications for federal funding (e.g., applications to federal agencies) and indirect applications for such funding (e.g., applications to state agencies that will subaward federal funds).

OJP seeks this information to help avoid any inappropriate duplication of funding. Leveraging multiple funding sources in a complementary manner to implement comprehensive programs or projects is encouraged and is not seen as inappropriate duplication.

Applicants that have pending applications as described above are to provide the following information about pending applications submitted within the last 12 months:

- the federal or state funding agency
- the solicitation name/project name
- the point of contact information at the applicable funding agency.

Federal or State Funding Agency	Solicitation Name/ Project Name	Name/Phone/E-mail for Point of Contact at Funding Agency
DOJ/COPS	COPS Hiring Program	Jane Doe, 202/000-0000; jane.doe@usdoj.gov
HHS/ Substance Abuse & Mental Health Services Administration	Drug Free Communities Mentoring Program/ North County Youth Mentoring Program	John Doe, 202/000-0000; john.doe@hhs.gov

Applicants should include the table as a separate attachment, with the file name "Disclosure of Pending Applications," to their application. Applicants that do not have pending applications as described above are to include a statement to this effect in the separate attachment page (e.g., "[Applicant Name on SF-424] does not have pending applications submitted within the last 12 months for federally funded grants or subgrants (including cooperative agreements) that include requests for funding to support the same project being proposed under this solicitation and will cover the identical cost items outlined in the budget narrative and worksheet in the application under this solicitation.").

b. Timeline, see page 16.

c. Logic model, see page 16.

d. Résumés of all key personnel

e. Job descriptions outlining roles and responsibilities for all key positions

f. Letters of support/memoranda of understanding from partner organizations, see page 17.

g. Evidence of nonprofit status, e.g., a copy of the tax exemption letter from the Internal Revenue Service, if applicable.

h. Evidence of for-profit status, e.g., a copy of the articles of incorporation, if applicable.

8. **Financial Management and System of Internal Controls Questionnaire**

In accordance with 2 CFR 200.205, federal agencies must have in place a framework for evaluating the risks posed by applicants before they receive a federal award. To facilitate part of this risk evaluation, **all** applicants (other than an individual) are to download, complete, and submit this form.

9. **Disclosure of Lobbying Activities**

All applicants must complete this information. Applicants that expend any funds for lobbying activities are to provide the detailed information requested on the form Disclosure of Lobbying Activities (SF-LLL). Applicants that do not expend any funds for lobbying activities are to enter "N/A" in the text boxes for item 10 ("a. Name and Address of Lobbying Registrant" and "b. Individuals Performing Services").

How To Apply

Applicants must register in and submit applications through Grants.gov, a "one-stop storefront" to find federal funding opportunities and apply for funding. Find complete instructions on how to register and submit an application here. Applicants that experience technical difficulties during this process should call the Grants.gov Customer Support Hotline at **800-518-4726** or **606–545–5035**, 24 hours a day, 7 days a week, except federal holidays. Registering with Grants.gov is a one-time process; however, **processing delays may occur, and it can take several weeks** for first-time registrants to receive confirmation and a user password. OJP encourages applicants to **register several weeks before** the application submission deadline. In addition, OJP urges applicants to submit applications 72 hours prior to the application due date to allow time to receive validation messages or rejection notifications from Grants.gov, and to correct in a timely fashion any problems that may have caused a rejection notification.

OJJDP strongly encourages all prospective applicants to sign up for Grants.gov email notifications regarding this solicitation. If this solicitation is cancelled or modified, individuals who sign up with Grants.gov for updates will be automatically notified.

Note on file names and file types. Grants.gov only permits the use of certain specific characters in names of attachment files. Valid file names may include only the characters shown in the table below. Grants.gov is designed to reject any application that includes an attachment(s) with a file name that contains <u>any</u> characters not shown in the table below.

Characters	Special Characters		
Upper case (A – Z)	Parenthesis ( )	Curly braces { }	Square brackets [ ]
Lower case (a – z)	Ampersand (&)	Tilde (~)	Exclamation point (!)
Underscore (__)	Comma (,)	Semicolon (;)	Apostrophe (')
Hyphen (-)	At sign (@)	Number sign (#)	Dollar sign ($)
Space	Percent sign (%)	Plus sign (+)	Equal sign (=)
Period (.)	**When using the ampersand (&) in XML, applicants must use the "&" format.**		

Grants.gov is designed to forward successfully submitted applications to OJP's Grants Management System (GMS).

GMS does not accept executable file types as application attachments. These disallowed file types include, but are not limited to, the following extensions: ".com," ".bat," ".exe," ".vbs," ".cfg," ".dat," ".db," ".dbf," ".dll," ".ini," ".log," ".ora," ".sys," and ".zip." GMS may reject applications with files that use these extensions. It is important to allow time to change the type of file(s) if the application is rejected.

All applicants are required to complete the following steps:
OJP may not make a federal award to an applicant until the applicant has complied with all applicable DUNS and SAM requirements. If an applicant has not fully complied with the requirements by the time the federal awarding agency is ready to make a federal award, the federal awarding agency may determine that the applicant is not qualified to receive a federal award and use that determination as a basis for making a federal award to another applicant.

1. **Acquire a Data Universal Numbering System (DUNS) number.** In general, the Office of Management and Budget requires that all applicants (other than individuals) for federal funds include a DUNS number in their applications for a new award or a supplement to an existing award. A DUNS number is a unique nine-digit sequence recognized as the universal standard for identifying and differentiating entities receiving federal funds. The identifier is used for tracking purposes and validating address and point of contact information for federal assistance applicants, recipients, and subrecipients. The DUNS number will be used throughout the grant life cycle. Obtaining a DUNS number is a free, one-time activity. Call Dun and Bradstreet at 866–705–5711 to obtain a DUNS number or apply online at www.dnb.com. A DUNS number is usually received within 1-2 business days.

2. **Acquire registration with the System for Award Management (SAM).** SAM is the repository for standard information about federal financial assistance applicants, recipients, and subrecipients. OJP requires all applicants (other than individuals) for federal financial assistance to maintain current registrations in the SAM database. Applicants must be registered in SAM to successfully register in Grants.gov. Applicants must **update or renew their SAM registration annually** to maintain an active status.

Applicants cannot successfully submit their applications until Grants.gov receives the SAM registration information. **The information transfer from SAM to Grants.gov can**

take as long as 48 hours. OJP recommends that the applicant register or renew registration with SAM as early as possible.

Access information about SAM registration procedures here.

3. **Acquire an Authorized Organization Representative (AOR) and a Grants.gov username and password.** Complete the AOR profile on Grants.gov and create a username and password. Applicant organizations must use their DUNS number to complete this step. For more information about the registration process, go here.

4. **Acquire confirmation for the AOR from the E-Business Point of Contact (E-Biz POC).** The E-Biz POC at the applicant organization must log into Grants.gov to confirm the applicant organization's AOR. Note that an organization can have more than one AOR.

5. **Search for the funding opportunity on Grants.gov.** Use the following identifying information when searching for the funding opportunity on Grants.gov. The Catalog of Federal Domestic Assistance number for this solicitation is 16.540 titled *Juvenile Justice and Delinquency Prevention Allocation to States.* The funding opportunity number is OJJDP-2015-4217.

6. **Submit a valid application consistent with this solicitation by following the directions in Grants.gov.** Within 24–48 hours after submitting the electronic application, the applicant should receive two notifications from Grants.gov. The first will confirm the receipt of the application and the second will state whether the application has been successfully validated, or rejected due to errors, with an explanation. It is possible to first receive a message indicating that the application is received and then receive a rejection notice a few minutes or hours later. Submitting well ahead of the deadline provides time to correct the problem(s) that caused the rejection. **Important:** OJP urges applicants to submit applications **at least 72 hours prior** to the application due date to allow time to receive validation messages or rejection notifications from Grants.gov, and to correct in a timely fashion any problems that may have caused a rejection notification.

    Click here for further details on DUNS, SAM, and Grants.gov registration steps and timeframes.

Note: Duplicate applications. If an applicant submits multiple versions of the same application, OJJDP will review only the most recent system-validated version submitted. See Note on File Names and File Types under How To Apply.

Experiencing Unforeseen Grants.gov Technical Issues

Applicants that experience unforeseen Grants.gov technical issues beyond their control that prevent them from submitting their application by the deadline must contact the Grants.gov Customer Support Hotline or the SAM Help Desk to report the technical issue and receive a tracking number. The applicant must e-mail the Response Center at responsecenter@ncjrs.gov **within 24 hours after the application deadline** and request approval to submit their application. The e-mail must describe the technical difficulties, and include a timeline of the applicant's submission efforts, the complete grant application, the applicant's DUNS number, and any Grants.gov Help Desk or SAM tracking number(s).

Note: OJJDP does not automatically approve requests. After the program office reviews the submission and contacts the Grants.gov or SAM Help Desks to validate the reported technical issues, OJP will inform the applicant whether the request to submit a late application has been approved or denied. If OJP determines that the applicant failed to follow all required procedures, which resulted in an untimely application submission, OJP will deny the applicant's request to submit their application.

The following conditions are generally insufficient to justify late submissions:

- failure to register in SAM or Grants.gov in sufficient time
- failure to follow Grants.gov instructions on how to register and apply as posted on its website
- failure to follow each instruction in the OJP solicitation
- technical issues with the applicant's computer or information technology environment, including firewalls.

Notifications regarding known technical problems with Grants.gov, if any, are posted at the top of the OJP funding webpage**.**

E. Application Review Information

Selection Criteria

The following five selection criteria will be used to evaluate each application, with the different weight given to each based on the percentage value listed after each individual criteria. For example, the first criteria, Statement of the Problem, is worth 10 percent of the entire score in the application review process.

1. Statement of the Problem (10 percent)
2. Goals, Objectives, and Performance Measures (10 percent)
3. Project Design and Implementation (45 percent)
4. Capabilities and Competencies (25 percent)
5. Budget: complete, cost effective, and allowable (e.g., reasonable, allocable, and necessary for project activities). Budget narratives should generally demonstrate how applicants will maximize cost effectiveness of grant expenditures. Budget narratives should demonstrate cost effectiveness in relation to potential alternatives and the goals of the project.[3] (10 percent)

See What an Application Should Include, page 11, for the criteria that the peer reviewers will use to evaluate applications.

Review Process

OJP is committed to ensuring a fair and open process for awarding grants. OJJDP reviews the application to make sure that the information presented is reasonable, understandable, measurable, and achievable, as well as consistent with the solicitation.

---

[3] Generally speaking, a reasonable cost is a cost that, in its nature or amount, does not exceed that which would be incurred by a prudent person under the circumstances prevailing at the time the decision was made to incur the costs.

Peer reviewers will review the applications submitted under this solicitation that meet basic minimum requirements. For purposes of assessing whether applicants have met basic minimum requirements, OJP screens applications for compliance with specified program requirements to help determine which applications should proceed to further consideration for award. Although program requirements may vary, the following are common requirements applicable to all solicitations for funding under OJP grant programs:

- Applications must be submitted by an eligible type of applicant.
- Applications must request funding within the funding limitation set for this solicitation (if applicable).
- Applications must be responsive to the scope of the solicitation.
- Applications must include all items designated as "critical elements."
- Applicants will be checked against the General Services Administration's Excluded Parties List.

For a list of critical elements, see "What an Application Should Include" under Section D. Application and Submission Information.

OJJDP may use internal peer reviewers, external peer reviewers, or a combination, to assess applications meeting basic minimum requirements on technical merit using the solicitation's selection criteria. An external peer reviewer is an expert in the subject matter of a given solicitation who is not a current DOJ employee. An internal reviewer is a current DOJ employee who is well-versed or has expertise in the subject matter of this solicitation. A peer review panel will evaluate, score, and rate applications that meet basic minimum requirements. Peer reviewers' ratings and any resulting recommendations are advisory only, although their views are considered carefully. In addition to peer review ratings, considerations for award recommendations and decisions may include, but are not limited to, underserved populations, geographic diversity, strategic priorities, past performance under prior OJJDP and OJP awards, and available funding.

OJP reviews applications for potential discretionary awards to evaluate the risks posed by applicants before they receive an award. This review may include but is not limited to the following:

1. Financial stability and fiscal integrity.
2. Quality of management systems and ability to meet the management standards prescribed in the Financial Guide.
3. History of performance.
4. Reports and findings from audits.
5. The applicant's ability to effectively implement statutory, regulatory, or other requirements imposed on non-Federal entities.
6. Proposed costs to determine if the Budget Detail Worksheet and Budget Narrative accurately explain project costs, and whether those costs are reasonable, necessary, and allowable under applicable federal cost principles and agency regulations.

Absent explicit statutory authorization or written delegation of authority to the contrary, all final award decisions will be made by the Assistant Attorney General, who may consider factors including, but not limited to, peer review ratings, underserved populations, geographic diversity, strategic priorities, past performance under prior OJJDP and OJP awards, and available funding when making awards.

F. Federal Award Administration Information

Federal Award Notices

OJP award notification will be sent from GMS. Recipients will be required to log in; accept any outstanding assurances and certifications on the award; designate a financial point of contact; and review, sign, and accept the award. The award acceptance process involves physical signature of the award document by the authorized representative and the scanning of the fully-executed award document to OJP.

Administrative, National Policy, and Other Legal Requirements

If selected for funding, in addition to implementing the funded project consistent with the agency-approved project proposal and budget, the recipient must comply with award terms and conditions, and other legal requirements, including but not limited to OMB, DOJ, or other federal regulations that will be included in the award, incorporated into the award by reference, or are otherwise applicable to the award. OJP strongly encourages prospective applicants to review the information pertaining to these requirements **prior** to submitting an application. To assist applicants and recipients in accessing and reviewing this information, OJP has placed pertinent information on its Solicitation Requirements page of the OJP Funding Resource Center.

Note in particular the following two forms, which applicants must accept in GMS prior to the receipt of any award funds, as each details legal requirements with which applicants must provide specific assurances and certifications of compliance. Applicants may view these forms in the Apply section of the OJP Funding Resource Center and are strongly encouraged to review and consider them carefully prior to making an application for OJP grant funds.

- Certifications Regarding Lobbying; Debarment, Suspension and Other Responsibility Matters; and Drug-Free Workplace Requirements

- Standard Assurances

Upon grant approval, OJP electronically transmits (via GMS) the award document to the prospective award recipient. In addition to other award information, the award document contains award terms and conditions that specify national policy requirements[4] with which recipients of federal funding must comply; uniform administrative requirements, cost principles, and audit requirements; and program-specific terms and conditions required based on applicable program (statutory) authority or requirements set forth in OJP solicitations and program announcements, and other requirements that may be attached to appropriated funding. For example, certain efforts may call for special requirements, terms, or conditions relating to intellectual property, data/information-sharing or -access, or information security; or audit requirements, expenditures and milestones, or publications

---

[4] See generally 2 C.F.R. 200.300 (provides a general description of national policy requirements typically applicable to recipients of federal awards, including the Federal Funding Accountability and Transparency Act of 2006 (FFATA)).

and/or press releases. OJP also may place additional terms and conditions on an award based on its risk assessment of the applicant, or for other reasons it determines necessary to fulfill the goals and objectives of the program.

Prospective applicants may access and review the text of mandatory conditions OJP includes in all OJP awards, as well as the text of certain other conditions, such as administrative conditions, via Mandatory Award Terms and Conditions page of the OJP Funding Resource Center.

As stated above, OJJDP anticipates that it will make any award from this solicitation in the form of a cooperative agreement. Cooperative agreement awards include standard "federal involvement" conditions that describe the general allocation of responsibility for execution of the funded program. Generally-stated, under cooperative agreement awards, responsibility for the day-to-day conduct of the funded project rests with the recipient in implementing the funded and approved proposal and budget, and the award terms and conditions. Responsibility for oversight and redirection of the project, if necessary, rests with OJJDP. OJJDP's role will include the following tasks:

- reviewing and approving major work plans, including changes to such plans, and key decisions pertaining to project operations.

- reviewing and approving major project-generated documents and materials used in the provision of project services.

- providing guidance in significant project planning meetings and participating in project sponsored training events or conferences.

In addition to any "federal involvement" condition(s), OJP cooperative agreement awards include a special condition specifying certain reporting requirements required in connection with conferences, meetings, retreats, seminars, symposium, training activities, or similar events funded under the award, consistent with OJP policy and guidance on conference approval, planning, and reporting.

General Information about Post-Federal Award Reporting Requirements

Recipients must submit quarterly financial reports, semi-annual progress reports, final financial and progress reports, and, if applicable, an annual audit report in accordance with 2 CFR Part 200. Future awards and fund drawdowns may be withheld if reports are delinquent.

Special Reporting requirements may be required by OJP depending on the statutory, legislative or administrative obligations of the recipient or the program.

G. Federal Awarding Agency Contact(s)

For additional Federal Awarding Agency Contact(s), see the title page.

For additional contact information for Grants.gov, see the title page.

H. Other Information

Provide Feedback to OJP

To assist OJP in improving its application and award processes, we encourage applicants to provide feedback on this solicitation, the application submission process, and/or the application review/peer review process. Provide feedback to OJPSolicitationFeedback@usdoj.gov.

IMPORTANT: This e-mail is for feedback and suggestions only. Replies are **not** sent from this mailbox. If you have specific questions on any program or technical aspect of the solicitation, **you must** directly contact the appropriate number or e-mail listed on the front of this solicitation document. These contacts are provided to help ensure that you can directly reach an individual who can address your specific questions in a timely manner.

If you are interested in being a reviewer for other OJP grant applications, please e-mail your resume to ojppeerreview@lmbps.com. The OJP Solicitation Feedback email account will not forward your resume. **Note:** Neither you nor anyone else from your organization can be a peer reviewer in a competition in which you or your organization have submitted an application.

Application Checklist

OJJDP FY 2015 Police and Youth Engagement:
Supporting the Role of Law Enforcement in Juvenile Justice Reform

This application checklist has been created to assist in developing an application.

What an Applicant Should Do:

Prior to Registering in Grants.gov:
_____Acquire a DUNs Number (see page 21)
_____Acquire or renew registration with SAM (see page 21)
To Register with Grants.gov:
_____Acquire AOR and Grants.gov username/password (see page 22)
_____Acquire AOR confirmation from the E-Biz POC (see page 22)
To Find Funding Opportunity:
_____Search for the Funding Opportunity on Grants.gov (see page 22)
_____Download Funding Opportunity and Application Package
_____ Sign up for Grants.gov email notifications (optional) (see page 20)
_____Read Important Notice: Applying for Grants in Grants.gov
After application submission, receive Grants.gov email notifications that:
_____(1) application has been received,
_____(2) application has either been validated or rejected (see page 22)
If no Grants.gov receipt, and validation or error notifications are received:
_____contact OJJDP regarding experiencing technical difficulties (see page 22)

General Requirements:

_____Review the Solicitation Requirements in the OJP Funding Resource Center.

Scope Requirement:

_____The federal amount requested is within the allowable limit(s) of $400,000.

Eligibility Requirement:

_____Nonprofit or for-profit organization, including tribal nonprofit or for-profit organization.
_____Institution of higher education, including tribal institution of higher education.

What an Application Should Include:

_____Application for Federal Assistance (SF-424) (see page 11)
_____Project Abstract (see page 12)
_____Program Narrative (see page 12)
_____Budget Detail Worksheet and Narrative (see page 17)
_____Employee Compensation Waiver request and justification (see page 10)
_____Read OJP policy and guidance on conference approval, planning, and reporting
available here. (see page 10)
_____Disclosure of Lobbying Activities (SF-LLL) (see page 20)
_____Indirect Cost Rate Agreement (if applicable) (see page 18)

_____Applicant Disclosure of High Risk Status (see page 18)
_____Additional Attachments (see page 19)
      _____Applicant Disclosure of Pending Applications

      _____Logic model
      _____Timeline or milestone chart
      _____Résumés of all key personnel
      _____Job descriptions outlining roles and responsibilities for all key positions
      _____Letters of support/memoranda of understanding from partner organizations
      _____Evidence of nonprofit status, e.g., a copy of the tax exemption letter from the Internal Revenue Service. if applicable.
      _____Evidence of for-profit status, e.g., a copy of the articles of incorporation, if applicable.
_____ Financial Management and System of Internal Controls Questionnaire (see page 20)